Self-Discovery Journal for Milennials (Teens and Young Adults)

200 Questions and Writing Prompts to Find Yourself and the Things You Want to Do in Life

Dreamstorm Publications

A Gift for You

Most of the material I write about is centered on developing our inner selves. Thus, as you might've guessed, my readers are usually introverts. I can appreciate that because I'm an introvert myself. However, as an introvert, I'm also aware of our social shortcomings. This is why I have decided to gift you with some amazing material for your growth. By simply clicking the link below, you will have access to the *Introvert Survival Kit* and *Inward Thrive* Email Series for free. Visit the following site or click here for full access: http://bit.ly/introvertsk

This powerful bundle will help you make massive improvements in your social life. It contains 3 Ebooks and 2 articles:

- EBook 1: Making and Keeping Friends: Developing Friendships that Last a Lifetime in this Fast Paced World!
- EBook 2: How to Stop Worrying and Start Living Effectively In the 21st Century: An Updated Guide to Living Free of Worry in the Knowledge Era
- EBook 3: High Impact Communication: Tips on Getting Your Strongest Message Across in 1 Minute
- Article 1: How to Break the Cycle of Anxiety and Enjoy Social Situations
- Article 2: Be an Introvert and Have an Active Social Life

Along with the material, you will also get a lot of bonus gifts in the days to come. I'd recommend not missing out! Just go to: http://bit.ly/introvertsk

I also have a special invitation for those appreciate a good read. If you'd like to be part of the review process of many of our upcoming books (and receive free copies!), and click here: http://bit.ly/itadvancedreview I will send you details of what it entails through mail. Thanks!

Introduction

In the world of mass communication and information we're living, it's getting increasingly harder to connect with ourselves. Time spent before reflecting on our innermost desires and goals is being replaced by the scrolling down of our social media feeds. Connections and relationships with others are diminished to simple exchanges of text messages. Moments of self-reflection and self-discovery are replaced by reading countless '5 reasons you're a (insert adjective here)' articles. Deep in our hearts, we're aware of this disconnect we're living, but heck, we don't know how to stop.

This journal is a remedy to that problem.

A very wise person (Aristotle) once said, "Knowing yourself is the beginning of all wisdom". I couldn't agree more. Knowing yourself can give you a better idea of what it is you want in life at this moment, the kind of job you'd like to have (or if you'd like one at all- perhaps you're more entrepreneurially inclined), what kind of trips you want to take, what kind of activities you want to surround your life with, what kind of friends you'd like to have- etc. Knowing what it is you want is the first step to its acquirement.

This Self-Discovery Journal is designed to reconnect you with yourself through daily fun and thought-provoking journaling prompts. All 200 questions found inside this self-discovery journal will help you discover things about yourself in different areas of your life. Also, in every single page you will find a relevant quote filled with wisdom and optimism.

Welcome to this journal of you.

This Journal

Belongs to...

Your Personal Space:

Vision board or inspirational photos. Your choice.

Your Personal Space:

Vision board or inspirational photos. Your choice.

Day 1 ___/___/___

Short-term goals.

In order to achieve bigger goals, you must first set smaller ones, especially when you're just starting out. What are your short-term goals at the moment and in how long are you hoping to achieve them?

Day 2 ___/___/___

Travel abroad and experience other cultures.

Living life to the fullest includes stepping out of your comfort zone and meeting new people. List down four countries you would love visit someday and discuss why you find them interesting.

"One's destination is never a place, but always a new way of seeing things."
- Heny Miller

Day 3 ___/___/___

If our lifespan were 30, how would you spend it?

They say life begins at 40. But if you have just three short decades to live, how would you make it worth remembering?

Day 4 ___/___/___

A chance to meet a famous and influential person.

Many of us idolize a particular person; be it a famous artist or an influential icon. How can meeting a renowned individual be an essential experience to you?

"Be genuinely interested in everyone you meet and everyone you meet will be genuinely interested in you."
- Rasheed Ogunlaru

Day 5 ___/___/___

Finish up a book.

Have you had the chance to sit down and enjoy a good book while sipping a cup of coffee? Perhaps, you've always wished to do so but never had the luxury of time. What three books would you like to take time reading?

Day 6 ___/___/___

What lifts your spirit when you are down?

Some people prefer to go out and unwind, while some prefer to take their time until they finally have the courage to leap out of bed and face reality again. How do you make yourself feel better during the hard times?

"You have to grow from the inside out. None can teach you, none can make you spiritual. There is no other teacher but your own soul."
– *Swami Vivekananda*

Day 7 ___/___/___

Donate blood.

Someone, somewhere, is in need of blood for certain medical procedures. Why do you think donating blood is something that we should all try doing, at least once?

Day 8 ___/___/___

Volunteer for a cause.

Despite the urge to help other people – to volunteer in an orphanage or a nursing home, for example – we either do not have enough time or resources to actually put this desire into action. Given a chance, what particular cause would you like to support by becoming a volunteer?

"If compassion was the motivating factor behind all of our decision, would our world not be a completely place?"
– *Sheryl Crow*

Day 9 ___/___/___

Learn how to play a musical instrument.

While others have an innate talent in music, learning how to play a guitar, a cello, or any instrument is something that we can actually practice. What would you like to learn, if you have the chance?

Day 10 ___/___/___

Master a foreign language.

Although it is not always required, learning a particular language aside from your own could open up more opportunities for you. What language do you want to learn or have you always fancied using?

"If you talk to a man in a language he understands, that goes to his head. If you talk to him in his own language, that goes to his heart."
- Nelson Mandela

Day 11 ___/___/___

Be offline for at least two weeks.

In a world where taking selfies and food photos have become just regular things people do online, how would you spend a couple of weeks without the use of the internet?

Day 12 ___/___/___

Public speaking.

Speaking in front of a crowd is not everyone's strong suit. It requires a certain confidence to make people listen to what you have to say. Would you dare try this one?

"There are three things to aim at in public speaking: first, to get into your subject, then to get your subject into yourself, and lastly, to get your subject into the heart of your audience."
– Alexander Gregg

Day 13 ___/___/___

Master (one) multimedia software.

You don't have to be an IT professional to benefit from this. Acquiring even basic editing skills will give you an edge in the job market. What would you try?

Day 14 ___/___/___

Learn to sing or dance.

This isn't about learning the how to's of singing and dancing; it's about relieving your stress through music and movement. When was the last time you tried to loosen up?

"Loosen up, and everybody around you will you will also loosen up."
– Sam Walton

Day 15 ___/___/___

Share a significant story that inspires you.

Sometimes, amidst our tiring daily routine, we need a little push to remind us why we are working hard in the first place. There may be a personal story that makes you leap out of bed every morning. Share it, so other people may find inspiration, too.

Day 16 ___/___/___

Learning the hard way.

Everyone has their own share of mishaps; nevertheless, learning the hard way makes us wiser and more careful with every decision. What is one problem you've had in the past that constitutes to the person that you are today?

"Take chances, make mistakes. That's how you grow. Pain nourishes your courage. You have to fail in order to practice being brave."
-Mary Tyler Moore

Day 17 ___/___/___

Have you touched anyone's life in a positive way?

You don't need to deliberately influence people of your ways. But do you think you practice enough optimism to leave an impact in other people's lives?

Day 18 ___/___/___

Flashback: One year ago.

Think of anything that you could not do (or you've had a hard time doing) last year, that you can actually do now. How did you convince yourself to work on that?

"I am always doing that which I cannot do,
in order that I may learn how to do it?"
– Pablo Picasso

Day 19 ___/___/___

Develop a stronger relationship with your loved ones.

If there's anyone who would accept and love us unconditionally despite our shortcoming, that is our family. When was the last time you tried to catch up with them?

Day 20 ___/___/___

Are your friends for keeps?

As much as we enjoy meeting new people, the fact is, we are not getting any younger. We should have a set of real and good friends who will stick with us through good times and the bad. Tell me about yours.

"Many people will walk in and out of your life, but only true friends will leave footprints in your heart."
– Eleanor Roosevelt

Day 21 ___/___/___

On ditching fair-weathered friends.

Along with keeping your real friends, why is it necessary to let go of the toxic and unsupportive ones?

Day 22 ___/___/___

A (positive) trait you have always longed to have.

Would you like to be more forgiving? How about to be someone who can stretch his patience a lot especially at work? What is that one trait you've always wished to have and in what situation can you possibly use it?

"I look only to the good qualities of men. Not being faultless myself, I won't presume to probe into the faults of others."
– Mahatma Gandhi

Day 23 ___/___/___

Getting yourself geared up for another day.

Some people are having a hard time getting up for work, especially when the job doesn't excite them anymore. But they have to because that's what matured and responsible individuals do. How do you maintain a positive mindset on a daily basis?

Day 24 ___/___/___

Reconcile with someone you had a misunderstanding with.

Turning over a new leaf requires forgiveness; and forgiveness allows us to finally have the peace of mind we deserve. Think of that person whom you wanted to reconnect with.

"Mistakes are always forgivable, if one has the courage to admit them."
– *Bruce Lee*

Day 25 ___/___/___

Recollect a wonderful childhood memory.

They say getting where we aim to be wouldn't be possible without recognizing where we came from. Our childhood memories always have a way to remind us of who we really are. Share your best childhood story.

Day 26 ___/___/___

Your outlook in life at 15.

Many of us experience self-discovery at this stage; some even have their first major heart break. How did you view the world as a teenager?

"I don't know what better teenage life you could get than going around the world doing what you love to do."
– Anna Kournikova

Day 27 ___/___/___

Figure out how you would like to be remembered.

Some people wanted to be remembered for the legacy they left; what they do, what they advocate for. Others, however, simply want to be remembered as someone who lived his life to the fullest. Have you honestly thought of this?

Day 28 ___/___/___

Fast-forward: 10 years from now.

Perhaps one of the most clichéd self-question we've heard of, but seriously, how do you imagine yourself in 10 years time?

"Remember how far you've come, and you won't have to rely on a destiny for your future. It will come on your own."
– Shannon A. Thompson

Day 29 ___/___/___

Are you independent ☺ in all aspects?

Independence doesn't only focus on the financial matters, or the ability to sustain your own lifestyle without the help of others. Emotional independence is also an essential factor in being self-reliant.

Day 30 ___/___/___

Pain is part of the process.

Suffering and sacrifices are both necessary in order to achieve something. What phase in your life do you consider the most (or one of the most) painful and how did you come to terms with the sadness?

"Pain is a part of life; it is what makes us human. It shapes us the same as love and laughter. You don't have to forget, but you cannot let it destroy you. Conquer the pain, don't let it conquer you."
– Cale Bloskas

Day 31 ___/___/___

Important values to live by.

Appreciation, commitment, compassion – just some of the great values we should have in order to attain a joyous life. What 3 values are most important to you and how do you try to put them into practice?

Day 32 ___/___/___

Do something extreme.

Have you considered doing something radical in form of sports? Not everyone loves the thrill of taking risks, but what particular activity do you wish to do, say if you've gathered enough courage to try?

"I'm one of these people who like adrenaline and new things, like extreme sports. It makes me feel alive."
– Gisele Bundchen

Day 33 ___/___/___

Have your treated yourself lately?

How are you going to nail it at work if you do not reward yourself for your achievements? How are you supposed to give your best at home when you are always too exhausted because of the chores? Rewarding yourself every once in awhile is not a sin. When was the last time you get yourself pampered?

Day 34 ___/___/___

Your greatest talent / skill.

It could be cooking or painting; for some it is graphic designing or playing a musical instrument. What is your greatest skill and how did it become relevant to your daily life?

"When love and skill work together, expect a masterpiece."
– John Ruskin

Day 35 ___/___/___

Road trips to nowhere; sound at full blast.

Sometimes, we just want to escape for awhile, find tranquility somewhere else and take our mind off the monthly expenses and deadlines. Imagine yourself in a long drive, listening to your favorite music genre, with no particular plan in mind. Where are you probably heading?

Day 36 ___/___/___

Being too conscious hinders you from being happy.

You always feel bad for not having an ideal body figure; you're always too conscious about how you look in your dress. Insecurities hinder us from fully loving ourselves. When was the last time you did something so freely that it made you really happy?

"I think the reward for conformity is that everyone likes you except yourself."
- Rita Brown

Day 37 ___/___/___

Definition of happiness.

Some people find happiness in their children; others prefer to prioritize their career. Many people enjoy traveling while they're young, while some think being vigorous and healthy are good enough. How do you define your own happiness?

Day 38 ___/___/___

A mentor you look up to.

It could be a teacher in high school, or simply an elderly friend. Who do you consider your greatest life mentor and what advice from this person have you actually put into practice?

"The best way a mentor can prepare another leader is to expose him or her to other great people."
– *John C. Maxwell*

Day 39 ___/___/___

Non-negotiable standards.

As we get older, we discover the kind of things and people we'd like (and not like) to settle with. However, the standards we set for ourselves should be non-negotiable. What are the standards you follow in life, career and relationship-wise?

Day 40 ___/___/___

Self-satisfaction.

At this age, do you feel as though something isn't complete? Ponder on this and ask yourself: I am satisfied with everything I have?

"Be thankful for what you have; you'll end up having more. If you concentrate on what you don't have, you will never, ever have enough."
– Oprah Winfrey

Day 41 ___/___/___

Put your feelings into words.

Not everyone has the talent in writing, but you can always try. Sometimes, all it takes is a relaxing place with the perfect ambiance to set you in the right mood. What personal story, or insights, would you like to share?

Day 42 ___/___/___

Superstitions.

Have certain superstitions in your country actually hindered you from doing something you really like? Tell us more about it.

"Superstition is foolish, childish, primitive and irrational - but how much does it cost you to knock on wood?"
– Judith Viorst

Day 43 ___/___/___

Movies to watch in your lifetime.

List down at least 3 emotionally compelling movies you've seen that made you rethink about your life or situation. How can a movie be a good way to question your current life circumstance?

Day 44 ___/___/___

A subject you'd like to master.

It's never too late for someone who wanted to learn. What useful subject do you want to master if given a chance?

"I can't run forever. I decided to go back to school for my degree, because I know now there's more to life than track."
– Evelyn Ashford

Day 45 ___/___/___

Witness a child delivery process.

Child birth, as said many times, is the essence of being a woman. Having a child gives us a better outlook in life. It may seem a little odd, but would you consider witnessing one?

Day 46 ___/___/___

Long-term goals.

We work hard because we aim to buy our dream house, provide good education for our future children and the list just goes on. What are your long-term goals and what do you do in order to achieve them?

"Our goals can only be reached through a vehicle of a plan, in which we must fervently believe, and upon which we must vigorously act. There is no other route to success."
– Pablo Picasso

Day 47 ___/___/___

What makes your life exciting?

Our daily routine tends to be so predictable, so when we finally got a good set of activities lined up, we look forward to starting our day with much enthusiasm. What makes your life exciting at the moment?

Day 48 ___/___/___

Giving advice.

Long before you've grown to be the responsible individual that you are right now, you had been through a lot and learned things the hard way. What advice will you give a teenager in order for him to be on the right path as he matures?

"In life, you need many more things besides talent. Things like good advice and common sense."
– Hack Wilson

Day 49 ___/___/___

The best version of yourself.

Recognize your weaknesses and work on it. There is no end in making yourself better, it just continues until you feel secured and satisfied with where you are. How do you try to be better, or possibly be the best version of yourself?

Day 50 ___/___/___

Decision-making.

Look back at the toughest decision you had to make and recall the factors you considered during the decision-making process.

"Our daily decisions and habits have a huge impact upon both our levels of happiness and success."
– Shawn Achor

Day 51 ___/___/___

Regrets.

Everyone has made a decision they are not very proud of. In retrospect, what is your biggest regret and what could have caused this mistake?

Day 52 ___/___/___

Yourself as a leader.

What constitutes a good leader? And how do you see yourself as one?

"The art of communication is the language of leadership."
– James Humes

Day 53 ___/___/___

Importance of family.

Describe your relationship with your mother and father while you were growing up. How did their love and encouragement (or lack thereof) help you become who you are today?

Day 54 ___/___/___

Crying is good for the soul.

To release your emotion through crying is actually healthier than trying to keep it in. When was the last time you cried so hard and for what reason? How did it make you feel after?

"Crying is all right in its way while it lasts. But you have to stop sooner or later, and then you still have to decide what to do."
– C.S. Lewis

Day 55 ___/___/___

Your most favorite places.

When our stress level has become too much to bear, we all need to pause and breathe. Give at least 3 of your most favorite places to relax your mind – it doesn't have to be a beautiful vacation spot, but a place where you feel at peace.

Day 56 ___/___/___

Family traditions to pass down.

Every family follows a certain tradition. What particular belief would you like to be passed down to your family's youngest (and upcoming) generation?

"People are interested in family traditions and
I think a lot families can benefit from some of the ways that my parents dealt
with the challenges of raising four kids."
– Ralph Nader

Day 57 ___/___/___

Your best traits.

Do not be ashamed to acknowledge the good qualities that you have as an individual. Give at least 3 best traits that you have and how do they help you become better?

Day 58 ___/___/___

Acknowledge the bad.

As much as we'd like to keep it to ourselves, we should also acknowledge our personal shortcomings in order to act on it. What 3 not-so-good traits do you think you have and how are you working on them?

"What I am is how I came out. No one's perfect and you just have to accept your flaws and learn to love yourself."
– Kelly Brook

Day 59 ___/___/___

Work under pressure.

How good (or bad) are you in handling stress? Some people always needed emotional support while others seem to be really good at controlling their emotions. What about you?

Day 60 ___/___/___

How do you choose your friends?

You are probably at the stage where you can't afford wasting time with unworthy people. What are your personal standards in choosing friends? And how important it is to be with the good ones?

"The people you surround yourself with influence your behaviors, so choose friends who have healthy habits."
– Dan Buettner

Day 61 ___/___/___

Your life hero.

It could be your parents, or your favorite grandma who acted as your guardian every time your mom and dad had to go to work. Who is that person you consider your hero? Tell me more about him/her.

Day 62 ___/___/___

Retirement.

At what age do you see yourself finally retiring and what do you want to enjoy by this time?

"To enjoy a long, comfortable retirement, save more today."
– *Suze Orman*

Day 63 ___/___/___

Career goals.

What particular goals in your career do you wish to achieve, and how are you actually working on it?

Day 64 ___/___/___

Life outside work.

No matter how much we wanted to climb the corporate ladder, we should not compromise our personal space and enjoy other things aside from work. What non-work related topics or activities do you enjoy?

"I have learned that keeping my personal life outside of work is the easier, richer way to work."
– *Jennifer Carpenter*

Day 65 ___/___/___

Something new.

When was the last time you actually tried something new? It could be a travel destination, an activity and even food. So long as you tried to step out your normal routine or comfort zone.

Day 66 ___/___/___

Is the habit of comparing okay?

Do you sometimes find yourself comparing what you have with what others have? Be honest: how does this attitude help or affect you in general?

"Don't compare yourself with someone else's version of happy or thin.
Accepting yourself burns the most calories."
– Caroline Rhea

Day 67 ___/___/___

Honesty at its finest.

What's the most honest thing you have said to someone? Or has someone ever said to you? How essential honesty is when we interact with people?

Day 68 ___/___/___

Life lately.

Have you done something fun lately? If you haven't, do you remember the last time you did?

"Have fun. Do something nobody else had done before, or has done since."
– Paul Prudhomme

Day 69 ___/___/___

Your #MeTime.

When do you enjoy your personal space the most?

Day 70 ___/___/___

Enjoy so much that you'll lose track of time.

What activities do you love doing so much that you tend to not notice the time?

"Lighten up, just enjoy life, smile more, laugh more, and don't get so worked up about things."
– Kenneth Branagh

Day 71 ___/___/___

Passing on what you know.

If you could teach someone a skill you have or good at, what will it be?

Day 72 ___/___/___

What matters most?

When you're in your 60's and finally retired, what do you think are the things that would still matter, and would matter most?

"Most of what matters in your life takes place in your absence."
– Salman Rushdie

Day 73 ___/___/___

What makes you smile?

What often makes you smile? What MADE you smile today?

Day 74 ___/___/___

Gratefulness.

This week alone, what are the things that you're grateful for?

"Let us be grateful to people who make us happy, they are the charming gardeners who make our souls blossom."
– *Marcel Proust*

Day 75 ___/___/___

Life lessons.

One lesson life has taught you just recently?

Day 76 ___/___/___

Leaving an impact.

What impact do you wish to leave in this world?

"Caring about others, running the risk of feeling, and leaving an impact on people, brings happiness."
– *Harold Kushner*

Day 77 ___/___/___

Ponder on this.

Amidst your everyday busy life, pause for a while and think: What are the things that you may have been missing?

Day 78 ___/___/___

Self-love.

What do you love most about yourself?

"We can climb mountains with self-love."
– Samira Wiley

Day 79 ___/___/___

Prove them wrong.

When was the last time someone held a false-belief about you but you successfully proved them wrong? Go into detail.

Day 80 ___/___/___

A big no-no.

What set of attitudes do you consider unpleasant? How do you deal with unpleasant/ill-mannered people in general?

"People may hear your words, but they feel your attitude."
– John C. Maxwell

Day 81 ___/___/___

What makes you unique?

Every individual is different from others. What are you made of?

Day 82 ___/___/___

What have you been up to?

Describe your life in the past 6 months. Were you able to enjoy most of it, or probably spent more time sitting in front of your work desk?

"Enjoy life at the fullest. Sometimes you realize that money isn't everything."
– Rey Mysterio

Day 83 ___/___/___

What is love?

But most importantly, what and who do you think of when you hear this word (love)?

Day 84 ___/___/___

To be loved in return.

We know that love should grow naturally and is not something that we should dictate people about. But, if you have the chance to decide, how would you like to be loved?

"Love is when the other person's happiness is more important than your own."
– H. Jackson Brown, Jr.

Day 85 ___/___/___

Finding inspiration.

Without enough motivation, it is usually difficult to start doing things, let alone finish them. When and how do you find inspiration to do your work (or hobbies)?

Day 86 ___/___/___

Hold on or let go?

Whether it is about relationships or a job we really love, deciding whether to hold or let go is no easy feat. When do you know if it is the right time?

"People have a hard time letting go of their suffering. Out of a fear of the unknown, they prefer suffering that is familiar"
– Thich Nhat Hanh

Day 87 ___/___/___

Finding treasure online.

The internet can be a cruel world. But have you ever found anything online that was actually worth learning or sharing?

Day 88 ___/___/___

Money isn't everything.

Tell me something that money, no matter how big the amount is, cannot buy. How do you find happiness despite the lack of money?

"Not everything is for sale; not everything is about money."
– Martin Bouygues

Day 89 ___/___/___

Beyond the titles.

Beyond the names and the titles that people gave you – more than being a wife or a husband, a daughter or a son, who are you?

Day 90 ___/___/___

Everything's possible.

Can you think of a time when something you thought was impossible, actually happened? Like getting your dream job or having the chance to travel abroad. How exactly did it happen? / did you make it happen?

"When you're surrounded by people who share a passionate commitment around a common purpose, anything is possible."
– Howard Schultz

Day 91 ___/___/___

Home is where the heart is.

But what is home for you in the first place? How do you know that you're home?

Day 92 ___/___/___

Know what you deserve.

Was there a time when you had to settle for less? How did it work for you?

"The minute you settle for less than you deserve, you get even less than you settled for."
– Maureen Dowd

Day 93 ___/___/___

In choosing friends.

We are not getting any younger; we should be with positive people, we should be with friends that have a positive effect in our lives. How do you choose your friends?

Day 94 ___/___/___

Perception of beauty.

What makes a person beautiful – inside and out?

"A beautiful person is someone who stays true to themselves and their spirit; someone who is self-confident and can make you smile."
– Helena Christensen

Day 95 ___/___/___

What makes you proud?

What fills your heart with so much joy?

Day 96 ___/___/___

Finding peace.

We all feel the need to escape from our daily, busy life once in a while. Where or with whom do you find peace?

"You'll never find peace of mind until you listen to your heart."
— George Michael

Day 97 ___/___/___

Changes.

Are you afraid of changes? How do you think your life would be if you're living it differently?

Day 98 ___/___/___

Losing a loved one.

Have you ever lost a loved one? It could be a family member or a friend so dear to you. How did you come to terms with the sadness?

"Every human walks around with a certain kind of sadness. They may not wear it on their sleeves, but it's there if you look deep."
– *Taraji P. Henson*

Day 99 ___/___/___

Silent treatment.

Sometimes, being silent conveys more messages than words. When do you think it is better not to say anything than let your emotions get the best of you?

Day 100 ___/___/___

Success

How do you measure success? Who do you want to share your success with?

"Success is never final, failure is never fatal. It's courage that counts."
– John Wooden

Day 101 ___/___/___

Today always matters.

How will the present time matter decades from now, when you are a retired person just wishing to enjoy the rest of your life?

Day 102 ___/___/___

Lending a hand

Have you helped someone in need recently?

"Prayer indeed is good,
but while calling on the gods a man should himself lend a hand."
– *Hippocrates*

Day 103 ___/___/___

How are you, really?

How's life treating you lately? And how are you trying to cope with it?

Day 104 ___/___/___

Scariest moment.

What has been the scariest moment you faced in life so far? How were you able to overcome this phase, and such fear?

"Things are never quite as scary when you've got a best friend."
– Bill Watterson

Day 105 ___/___/___

Lessons and changes.

What is the life lesson you've learned recently that actually changed your mindset about things?

Day 106 ___/___/___

Music is power.

Is there a particular song that makes you feel empowered?

"Where words fail, music speaks."
– Hans Christian Andersen

Day 107 ___/___/___

The power of words.

What is the nicest thing someone has ever said to you? Something that made you feel good about yourself, or inspired you to do better.

Day 108 ___/___/___

Yes, the power of words.

On the other hand, what is the meanest comment or criticism you've ever received from someone? How did it affect the way you look at yourself?

"Words have no power to impress the mind
without the exquisite horror of their reality."
– Edgar Allan Poe

Day 109 ___/___/___

Peer pressure.

What is the greatest peer pressure you've felt and how did you manage it?

Day 110 ___/___/___

White lies.

Would you rather hurt someone by telling him the truth OR give him temporary comfort by telling him what he wants to hear?

"White lies always introduce others of a darker complexion."
– William S. Paley

Day 111 ___/___/___

Hurting other's feeling.

Have you ever done something that unintentionally hurt someone else's feelings? Share your story.

Day 112 ___/___/___

Failed chances.

What is that one chance you regret not taking?

"You will never change your life, until you change something you do daily."
-Unknown

Day 113 ___/___/___

Being happy.

What made you smile today? What made you happy this week?

Day 114 ___/___/___

Perseverance.

What is something you want so bad that you will never, ever give up and why is that so?

"Perseverance is the hard work you do after you get tired of doing the hard work you already did."
– Newt Gingrich

Day 115 ___/___/___

On being uncomfortable.

What kind of thing, activity or person makes you really uncomfortable? How do you handle awkward, uncomfortable situations?

Day 116 ___/___/___

Being a mentor

If you could mentor someone, who would that person be and what exactly are you going to teach him/her? It could be about anything.

"The delicate balance of mentoring someone is not creating them in your own image, but giving them the opportunity to create themselves."
– Steven Spielberg

Day 117 ___/___/___

De-stress

What's the best way you know in relieving your stress?

Day 118 ___/___/___

Who makes you feel good about yourself?

One reason why we should be smart in choosing our friends is because we shouldn't entertain so much negativity in our life. Who are the people that send you positive vibes every time and make you feel good about yourself?

"Do and act on what you believe to be right, and you'll wake up the next morning feeling good about yourself."
– Janet Reno

Day 119 ___/___/___

One thing that most people do not know about you.

It could be a talent in music, or in cooking; perhaps you have a habit that many people may find unusual. What is something about yourself that many people around you are not really aware of?

Day 120 ___/___/___

Social Interaction

When was the last time you went out, socialized with people, and actually made new friends? Why is meeting new people once in a while important?

"Girls enjoy complex social interaction. Their verbal skills - and their delight in using them - develop earlier than boys'."
– Brenda Laurel n

Day 121 ___/___/___

The random free hours.

Sometimes, amidst the day, we'll get a random free time – say an hour or three. How do you want to spend this?

Day 122 ___/___/___

Because we are mature and responsible individuals.

Sometimes, we have to do something again and again no matter how much we hate it, just because it's part of the job or part of being an independent individual. What are the things you do over again that you actually hate doing?

"The greatest gifts you can give your children are the roots of responsibility and the wings of independence."
– Denis Waitley

Day 123 ___/___/___

Someone who you find really impressive.

Who is that person whom you admire for his skills or talent? Is there anyone who impresses you so much, and for what reason? (someone you know personally and not a celebrity or famous person)

Day 124 ___/___/___

Looking for a significant other.

Looking for a lifetime partner is no easy task. You have to set a standard and not settle for less because you are – hopefully – going to spend the rest of your life with this person. What qualities are you looking for in a partner?

"The most important quality in a partner is a sense of humor."
– Clare Balding

Day 125 ___/___/___

Feeling lost and alone.

Have you, in the past 3 years, ever felt lost or alone? This happens to everyone. But how did you come to terms with that emptiness? How were you able to get back on your feet?

Day 126 ___/___/___

Missing an opportunity.

Our decisions were not quite good when we were young. What is one great opportunity you think you missed out when you were a lot younger?

"We've all got a black book of missed opportunities."
– Jim Broadbent

Day 127 ___/___/___

Aside from money, what other things have your acquired from your job?

Some are thankful for the friendship they found; others for the fun experience, but what about you? What are the things that you gained and why are you thankful for them?

Day 128 ___/___/___

Quality time with the family.

What particular activity do you enjoy doing with your family, especially when you are trying to catch up after several busy weeks (or months)?

"I don't think quantity time is as special as quality time with your family."
– Rebe McEntire

Day 129 ___/___/___

What do you appreciate most about your leaders at work?

Good leaders inspire us to do better at work. As an individual, what are the things that you like or appreciate about your seniors?

Day 130 ___/___/___

On making yourself better.

Ponder on 3 failures you had recently. It could be about your relationship with someone, your job, or friends. What did you learn from these failures and how did they help in shaping you to become a better person?

"Failure happens all the time. It happens every day in practice. What makes you better is how you react to it."
– Mia Hamm

Day 131 ___/___/___

Keeping your motivation.

Everyone, at some point, loses his or her motivation to keep going – especially when our routine gets very predictable. When was the last time you lost your motivation to do things and how did you overcome such phase?

Day 132 ___/___/___

Work-life balance

We must first get our priorities straight in order to acquire the work-life balance we want. How are you trying to work on this?

"It's important to have balance in your life between work and play."
– Bobby Flay

Day 133 ___/___/___

Has someone every disheartened you?

... to the point where you lose your self-confidence and even questioned your own ability to accomplish things?

Day 134 ___/___/___

Changes in perspective and mindset.

How different is your life perspective today to the way you view things 3 to 5 years ago? What do you think happened that gave you a better mindset towards the things that surround you?

"I'm always going to try to win with a positive mindset."
– Brock Osweiler

Day 135 ___/___/___

Happiness in the workplace.

How happy are you right now in your job? What are the things at work that make you happy in the first place?

Day 136 ___/___/___

Faith renewed.

What act of kindness (even as simple as a gesture) have you witnessed that renewed your faith in humanity?

"Faith is taking the first step even when you don't see the whole staircase."
– Martin Luther King, Jr.

Day 137 ___/___/___

Physical changes.

Many people consider having a new look because it makes them feel like having a new outlook in life, too. Would you like to go on a makeover? Perhaps a new haircut or hair color would help you feel refreshed.

Day 138 ___/___/___

What is the biggest hindrance that stands your way at the moment?

It could be something that hinders you from leaving the job you don't like, or going on a solo trip abroad. Anything that stops you from doing what you should've already done before.

"A monk's extraordinary patience can be a hindrance
to desperate decision-making."
– Harsha Bhogle

Day 139 ___/___/___

What makes you feel secure?

Do you need someone else to give you that feeling of security? Or are you independent enough to feel secured on your own?

Day 140 ___/___/___

What is your favorite sound of nature?

Many people enjoy the sound of waves, while others simply enjoy the sound of rain while looking at the window pane. What about you?

"I just really dig feeling subservient to nature. It brings me a peace and calm. Kind of like a Faustian thing, I think."
– Neko Case

Day 141 ___/___/___

What is your favorite smell?

This question could be a little tricky. It isn't just about the smell of food, or your favorite fragrance. Sometimes, even the smell of a newly brewed coffee can trigger a certain emotion in you; smell can bring back memories. So what is your favorite one?

Day 142 ___/___/___

New memories.

What recent memories can make you smile?

"I believe that without memories there is no life, and that our memories should be of happy times."
– Lee Radziwill

Day 143 ___/___/___

Laugh out loud.

When was the last time you laugh so hard? What was it about?

Day 144 ___/___/___

Let's talk about fear.

What is your biggest fear/phobia and how are you trying to overcome it?

"Tell us your phobias and we will tell you what you are afraid of."
– Robert Benchley

Day 145 ___/___/___

Regular communication.

How many friends do you try to keep in touch with regularly, and why these people in particular?

Day 146 ___/___/___

First impressions.

What is most people's usual first impression about you? Were they wrong about it? Go into detail.

"My belief is you have one chance to make a first impression."
– Kevin McCarthy

Day 147 ___/___/___

Are you more like your mom or your dad?

In what way do you resemble either your mother or father, in terms of attitude and behavior? Was it a good thing?

Day 148 ___/___/___

One bad habit that you want to break?

Are you a smoker? A drinker? Or a heavy sleeper that if affects your work at times? What kind of bad habit would you like to break and why is it so?

"Depending on what they are, our habits will either make us or break us. We become what we repeatedly do."
– Sean Covey

Day 149 ___/___/___

Near-death experience.

Have you ever had a near-death experience, or witness other people in grave danger?

Day 150 ___/___/___

Have you ever been so furious that you want to be violent?

Anger is a natural process. It is actually healthy to let it go, so long as you know how to control it. Have you ever been so angry that you want to yell or throw things?

"You will not be punished for your anger; you will be punished by your anger."
– Buddha

Day 151 ___/___/___

Realizations.

When did you fully realize that life, indeed, is short?

Day 152 ___/___/___

Societal pressure.

What is the biggest pressure that the society has ever put on you? How did you deal with the pressure?

"Society puts so much pressure on girls to look a certain way."
– Halima Aden

Day 153 ___/___/___

Just got lucky.

When was the last time you felt so lucky and for what reason?

Day 154 ___/___/___

When was the last time you argued with someone?

What was the reason behind the argument, and most importantly, how do you handle and settle this kind of misunderstanding?

"Silence is one of the hardest arguments to refute."
– Josh Billings

Day 155 ___/___/___

Ever regret not speaking up when you should have?

Sometimes we're scared of getting embarrassed that we choose to stay silent even when we know we needed to speak up. Have this ever happened to you?

Day 156 ___/___/___

Who is your best friend?

And why do you consider this person as one?

"My best friend is the one who brings out the best in me."
– Henry Ford

Day 157 ___/___/___

Who is that one person you are not comfortable with?

What could be the reason for this? Have you two had a misunderstanding in the past? Or for some reason, you just don't click at all?

Day 158 ___/___/___

How do you define comfortable living?

How do you measure being comfortable with life? Is it based solely on your financial stability or do you actually consider other things?

"At the end of the day, whether or not those people are comfortable with how you're living your life doesn't matter. What matters is whether you're comfortable with it."
– *Phil McGraw*

Day 159 ___/___/___

How much time do you spend online?

And what online activities actually make you busy?

Day 160 ___/___/___

Having a family.

At what age or point in life would you like to build your own family? What factors do you need to consider first before having one?

"A woman can plan when to have her family and how to support a family."
– Kathleen Turner

Day 161 ___/___/___

Going back to school.

Were you able to finish your studies? If not, would you consider pursuing your education once again? What are your thoughts on people who wanted to go back to school despite the age?

Day 162 ___/___/___

How do you deal with a broken heart?

Yes, relationship-wise. How did you come to terms with the pain and managed to get back on your feet once again?

"Of course! It takes a lot of strength to mend a broken heart. Channelising energies into your work helps, but also to be able to accept situations for what they are instead of questioning them helps immensely."
– Deepika Padukone n

Day 163 ___/___/___

Material things

Happiness is beyond material things, but what is one thing you'd wish to buy for yourself that will make you really happy?

Day 164 ___/___/___

When the going gets tough.

When things are messy and your life seems so busy, who is that one person you approach to confide all your stress and worries?

"Be able to confide your innermost secrets to your mother and your innermost fears to your father."
– Marilyn vos Savant

Day 165 ___/___/___

That one dream you are ashamed of.

Do you have a very personal dream or goal that you don't share to anyone because it'll be embarrassing to let other people know about it? (Try to share without mentioning it directly, if you're not comfortable.)

Day 166 ___/___/___

Fitting in vs. being different.

Would you prefer to fit in, or follow what you desire and be different?

"The most basic human desire is to feel like you belong. Fitting in is important."
- Simon Sinek

Day 167 ___/___/___

Your happiness vs. your loved one's.

Would you give up your own happiness if it means making someone else – a loved one in particular – happy? Whatever your answer is, please try to go into detail.

Day 168 ___/___/___

The common good.

Are you willing to give up something you value very much in order to acquire the common good?

"There is no higher religion than human service. To work for the common good is the greatest creed."
– *Woodrow Wilson*

Day 169 ___/___/___

What makes you, you?

What makes you a unique individual?

Day 170 ___/___/___

Because it's hard to forget meaningful conversations.

Have you ever met someone – a colleague or just a random stranger, anyone – whom you had a really good conversation with? Like you've known the person for a long time because everything you shared with each other was just on point?

"I'm always for constructive conversation, meaningful conversation, not just words, but conversation."
– J. B. Bickerstaff

Day 171 ___/___/___

Personal interaction in the future.

Many people (unintentionally) stopped having real interactions with others simply because we can now virtually hangout with just anyone you like, online. How do you see the way we would communicate with each other in the distant future?

Day 172 ___/___/___

Have you ever had a great conversation with a complete stranger?

What did you talk about? How did the conversation go despite the fact that you are strangers to each other?

"Smile at a stranger. See what happens."
– Patti LuPone

Day 173 ___/___/___

Facing challenges.

Challenges do not have to be something amazing. What do you think are the normal, day-to-day challenges that people face?

Day 174 ___/___/___

Future challenges.

Considering everything we know at this point, what do you think are the challenges that the future generation will face?

"Natural selection will not remove ignorance from future generations."
– Richard Dawkins

Day 175 ___/___/___

On dating:

What is your opinion on blind dates?

Day 176 ___/___/___

Know the difference.

Consider this: With all the responsibilities we face on a daily basis, are you actually living your life, or merely surviving?

"If you can't get excited about living life, then what are you doing?"
– Hill Harper

Day 177 ___/___/___

Passing on family values.

What values have your parents taught you that you ought to pass on to your (future) children?

Day 178 ___/___/___

The right career path.

If given the chance, would you rather put up your own business or just climb up the corporate ladder?

"The word career is a divisive word. It's a word that divides the normal life from business or professional life."
– Grace Paley

Day 179 ___/___/___

Having the right set of traits.

What traits do you think a good employee or entrepreneur should posses?

Day 180 ___/___/___

Because we'll do everything for a good friend.

It's not like we're counting the times we lend a hand, but what is the biggest thing you've done just to help a friend?

"To help a friend in need is easy, but to give him your time is not always opportune."
– Charlie Chaplin

Day 181 ___/___/___

Blending in.

Of course, it is good to have a good sense of individuality. But what adjustments have you done / or sometimes do in order to blend in?

Day 182 ___/___/___

Investing in good health?

Why is it really important to invest in good health? Especially when you've got so much life plans ahead of you?

"Good health and good sense are two of life's greatest blessings."
– Publilius Syrus

Day 183 ___/___/___

What kind of intelligence do you want to acquire?

Would you rather be logical-mathematical? Or perhaps be musically-inclined? Do you want to be very articulate in expressing yourself, thus linguistically talented? What kind of intelligence would you like to acquire and why?

Day 184 ___/___/___

Public display of affection.

When in public places, how much expressiveness and affection is actually too much?

"Love is not to be purchased, and affection has no price."
– St. Jerome

Day 185 ___/___/___

Attraction vs. love.

In your own experience or understanding, what is the difference between being attracted to someone and being in love?

Day 186 ___/___/___

Love at first sight.

Very few people are lucky enough to have experienced this, but do you think it's really possible to fall in love on the first meeting?

"Love at first sight is easy to understand; it's when two people have been looking at each other for a lifetime that it becomes a miracle."
– Sam Levenson

Day 187 ___/___/___

Love amidst the culture differences.

How can we possibly express love and respect to each other despite the differences in culture and beliefs we grew up with?

Day 188 ___/___/___

Music is a good motivator.

What songs or type of music do you listen to when you need some motivation?

"Music expresses that which cannot be said and on which it is impossible to be silent."
– *Victor Hugo*

Day 189 ___/___/___

Personality.

What kind of personality do you normally get along with easily?

Day 190 ___/___/___

Valuing one's privacy.

How much and how do you value your own privacy?

"Once you've lost your privacy,
you realize you've lost an extremely valuable thing."
– Billy Graham

Day 191 ___/___/___

Sharing your most valued privacy.

When and with whom are you willing to share your privacy?

Day 192 ___/___/___

When do you prefer to be alone?

And what do you do to enjoy being alone?

"Each time I think I've created time for myself, along comes a throwback to disrupt my private space."
- Wole Soyinka

Day 193 ___/___/___

Responsibilities.

What are some of your responsibilities as an individual? How do you to fulfill them?

Day 194 ___/___/___

Keeping secrets?

Are you good or comfortable in keeping secrets? Or would you rather not know any secret at all because it makes you uneasy?

"To keep your secret is wisdom; but to expect others to keep it is folly."
- Samuel Johnson

Day 195 ___/___/___

Sharing secrets.

Are you willing to share any of your success secrets in order to help someone who is struggling to get back on his feet?

Day 196 ___/___/___

Putting on pressure.

Do you think always reminding your children to study hard so they can be successful in the future is a form of pressure? Have you ever felt pressured as a child?

"There is such pressure on kids these days to be the best at everything."
- Shirley Henderson

Day 197 ___/___/___

Measuring success through money.

Many people are being judged based on what they do and do not have. Why do you think many people use money as a basis of how successful they are?

Day 198 ___/___/___

How did this era change your life?

How did the internet and social media change the way you live in the past years?

"Now is the era of intellect, information and the Internet."
- Lech Walesa

Day 199 ___/___/___

What is the biggest transition you have gone through?

For some it is landing on their first job; for others it could be marriage. But what about you, what do you consider the turning point of your life?

Day 200 ___/___/___

Why do you think transitions are important?

What can we actually acquire from these life transitions in the first place?

"Any transition is easier if you believe in yourself and your talent."
- Priyanka Chopra

"Stay hungry, stay foolish."
— Steve Jobs

Made in the USA
Columbia, SC
12 August 2020